Just a *Life* Story

Just a *Life* Story

Kaity Ford

gatekeeper press
Tampa, Florida

The views and opinions expressed in this book are solely those of the author and do not necessarily reflect the views or opinions of Gatekeeper Press. Gatekeeper Press is not to be held responsible for and expressly disclaims responsibility for the content herein.

JUST A LIFE STORY

Published by Gatekeeper Press
7853 Gunn Hwy., Suite 209
Tampa, FL 33626
www.GatekeeperPress.com

Copyright © 2023 by Kaity Ford

All rights reserved. Neither this book, nor any parts within it may be sold or reproduced in any form or by any electronic or mechanical means, including information storage and retrieval systems, without permission in writing from the author. The only exception is by a reviewer, who may quote short excerpts in a review.

Library of Congress Control Number: 2023934935

ISBN (paperback): 9781662938733
eISBN: 9781662938740

Foreword

JUST A LIFE STORY is a purpose-filled book to engage the reader to a real, raw testimony. In what were some of the deepest pains and struggles in life, Kaity talks about how God helped guide her through, and journey into seeing the testimony on the other side of the circumstance. This book will encourage you to walk through your trials continuing to keep your eyes fixed on the fact that God is STILL good, and He is always greater.

—KIRSTE WEGELE
Head Worship Leader at Northern Colorado Cowboy Church

Chapter One

AS I SAT DOWN at the ladies' luncheon for Hope Haven Rwanda, I had no idea I was about to be sent on an adventure into my past. The three ladies sitting next to me, I had never met before. We were in the midst of small talk when one of the ladies looked at me and said, "Now tell me about yourself, Kaity."

I paused for a moment. *Tell her about me?* I laughed inside because it had been quite a year, but then I thought to myself, *Actually, it has been quite a life.*

* * *

I was born in late September 1989 in Colorado. My earliest memories are of a small mountain town called Leadville, where I lived with my mother, a dental hygienist, and my father, the town carpenter. Soon, my little brother joined my world. I was not certain I had asked for him at first, but after not much time at all, I grew to love the little rascal. Mountain life was fun for a kid. My father built me a swing set and would dig out every foot of fallen snow so that I could get a full swing in.

Life was very simple—as simple as the town we lived in, it seemed. My little brother had arrived right in time for the town's living Nativity event, held at the small church we attended. Yes, that's correct—my brother was born just in time to be Jesus. That, of course, made my mom Mary and my carpenter father Joseph—a beautiful picture of perfection. One thing, though: There was this person called me. I was cast as the carpenter's assistant or something.

Well, that's just great, I thought to myself. I was the center of attention until, apparently, I became the big sister or random carpentry assistant of Jesus Himself. Needless to say, I was less than impressed with this new little savior of the world, but he was pretty cute, I guess.

We lived in Leadville for a few more years until my mom could no longer take the snow. We moved down the hill to a town called Castle Rock. At that point, Castle Rock consisted of an outlet mall and some horse pastures. I enjoyed my new surroundings, I guess. I did miss the snow and the trees, but at least down here, I was not known as Jesus's assistant.

I started at a Christian school after a brief stint of homeschooling. I am sure my mother was quite excited to send me to school after that one homeschooling year. To say I was an easy student to teach would be a lie. I had a level of sarcasm and bullheadedness even at that young age, which people who knew me back then still marvel at to this day. I had wonderful teachers, although school was never my strong suit. I had major issues with dyslexia. I struggled with reading and writing to the point that I had specialty classes and glasses to help my eyes focus. These were not my favorite things. Also, I was a bit of a chunky kid, and it seemed that the embarrassment never ended as I was called on to read aloud in class. The fact was that I could not do it, not like the other kids anyway, so I decided that I hated reading and writing. My parents put a great deal of value on education and academic achievement, which was a large load to carry. I went on doing my very best, and I was able to make acceptable grades for a while, anyway.

Life was good. I was doing well in school. I was doing well on the swim team. I was just doing well in general. Our family seemed happy and thriving in those days, but good times have a way of ending abruptly. I remember the night my parents sat my brother and me down at the table to tell us the news that my father had been diagnosed with cancer. My little mind could not even begin to understand the implications of what I was being told. I was only eight years old, after all. All I knew was my dad had to go to the doctor a lot coming up, and the Happy Meal in front of me was getting cold.

The first thing I felt I needed to do was to call my teacher at the time, Mrs. Burral. "Oh my Lord," she exclaimed. The sound of shock and fear in her voice was the first indication I had that maybe this was a bad place to be. My mom took over the conversation from there, explaining to my teacher that a few nights before, she and my dad had lain down for bed. She had noticed that one side of his stomach was higher than the other and very firm. She had immediately told my father that he needed to be seen, and he'd gone in the very next day. After many tests and analyses of my dad's symptoms, it had been determined he had a very large tumor growing from one of the vertebrae in his back. There was much hope and optimism, however, because it did appear to be operable. As that phone call ended, I began to understand that this was not good news at all and that life was about to be very different.

The surgery took eight hours or so. Well, I visited the gift shop in the hospital about eight times, anyway, and I figured that was about every hour. It seemed like forever, watching my mom's face try to hide the fear with bravery for my brother and me. Finally, the doctor came out to tell us that they had successfully removed an eight-pound tumor the size of a football from my dad's abdominal cavity. The other good news was that they were able to shave into it a bit and not remove the vertebrae that it was attached to, so my dad would not be paralyzed from the waist down. I did not realize that was a concern at that point, but now the many conversations I had been around to listen to but not directly told personally made a lot more sense.

"You can't take a man's legs from him," or "I have been a great runner my whole life, and I can't give that up," Dad would say on phone calls to many concerned citizens. It appeared that the storm was over now; internal radiation had been performed, and the tumor was gone. Now all that was left was recovery.

My dad had a scar from the bottom of his ribs all the way to his leg, and he looked pretty rough, but I could still recognize my superman, strong as he ever was, just knocked down a little. *He will be back up soon though*, I told myself. A few weeks and at least one hundred lasagnas provided by the wonderful ladies of our church later, my dad was back up and back to work.

His big job as a homebuilder was a great fulfillment to my dad, but also a great time-consumer. He would leave for work before I was awake for the day and arrive back home after bed most weekdays, but that would allow time on weekends for him to coach all our sports and hang with us. I had missed him while he was in recovery, but finally, things were normal. The family was fine, and we were back to life again.

I was right about that: things were normal again. My dad was in clinical remission, and we were back to normal: school, work, sports, and church life. I went through my third- and fourth-grade years pretty easily. I was doing better in school and had started playing basketball, with Dad coaching me all the way as he did with all the sports my brother and I played. I had been given an opportunity to start working with a local hunting dog kennel, helping with most aspects of that business, from training dogs to breeding to puppy rearing. It quickly became my favorite part of my young life, and I was soon able to purchase a female dog of my own named Sidney. The plan was to breed her and use the profits to save for my college education. I thought there was nothing better in life than being a part of the hunting dog world and figured I would do this work for the rest of my life.

The day then came when, after two awesome years, the bottom fell out once more. My dad had gone in for some scans, and though we had been told that the likelihood of the cancer coming back was almost none, it was back. It was a million-to-one odds. This time it would not be as easy as surgery and then back to life. We started chemotherapy for my dad, but the cancer was still slowly growing. It seemed that no matter how many surgeries or medications we threw at it, this time it would take him.

This was a slow, painful reality for our family, and it just seemed to get harder and harder. My dad became a very angry man. He began staying at work later and later to run away from his real life. It led to multiple affairs, one of which was pretty serious, to the point that my brother and I personally knew her. It was strange, I thought to myself, that this friend of my father would show up after his surgeries, and when she would walk into the room, I, my brother, and my mother would leave the room until she left and then return to the bedside. I was confused by it, to say the least. I was young, but I knew something was wrong with this situation.

A great hatred began to grow in my heart for this lady. Did she not see we were already losing the protector and provider of our family? Did it even matter to her, or why was she even here? These questions were never really answered; they only opened the door to other questions. Why was my mom allowing this? Was this actually okay? Was this really how my last days with my dad should be remembered? Well, the final terribly hard days turned into terribly hard years. There were occasional good times on a family vacation or when a litter of my dog's puppies was born. It was something that I could smile about and remember how life used to be, but then reality would sneak back in and smack me again.

I was fifteen when the last of the last days were finally upon us. Dad was no longer able to keep any food down or do anything, really. The days of working hard and coaching sports were long gone. My mom was the working one now. She would work to financially cover us and then spend the rest of her days as a caregiver for my dad. On days that my mom was at work, my little brother—who was in sixth grade—would run home every day, fearing he would find Dad dead on the couch. After finding him fine, he would empty Dad's puke bucket, then give him some medicine and start his homework.

I was checked out by this point, spending as much time as possible away from my house. I was in high school now, so there were many options for staying out—from friends to sports to anything at all that I could find. I would stay as far as possible from the crashing of my world. If I could find nothing to do, I would go run with my dog Earl, one of the pups from Sidney's litter. We would run six or seven miles, then walk in the door to hear my dad getting sick again, and we would turn right around and run another six or seven miles. Anything to stay gone.

The call I had known was coming finally came. I was at a theme park with my friends when my mom's voice on the other end of the line told me, "We had to call for hospice to come pick Dad up. Do you want to come home?"

Come home? What home? I thought to myself. "No, I will just stay gone. Plus, I'll go see him tomorrow," I said.

I called my dad later that evening, and he told me something about a sports team he was watching that did not make much sense, but he was in kidney failure, so I didn't think much of it. That was the last time I would speak with my father on the phone, because I could not and would not stay home. He languished away, unable to speak or eat or drink, for seven long days in hospice. Early on the seventh morning, we—my brother and I—were taken by my nana up to see him. A lady was getting into her car in the parking lot of the hospice, and she noticed us walking in. She turned around with a large grin on her face and asked me, "Are you here for Fred?"

"Yes," I said with a slight bit of hope that maybe some prayer somewhere had worked and maybe he was better or something.

But she said, "Well, you're too late; he is dead," and she got in her car and left.

Standing there shocked and completely broken, all I could think was, *Why was she smiling like that?* My superman was gone. The next few days went as expected with the viewing and funeral and all the death things.

"He fought the hospice," my brother recounted later. "He didn't want to go; he didn't want to die."

I did know that was true—he fought a very long, hard battle for eight years to live and to see us live. In those last days, he repented to my mom for all the terrible things he had done in their marriage. He also had an opportunity to repent to the Lord, and I believe he is in heaven to this day. Somehow, though, the sting was so great I could not seem to get away from the pain. I had learned to run away from pain, and I was great at it.

Chapter Two

LIFE WENT ON. At this point I was a sophomore in high school. I still had my friends, sports, and dogs, so I should be fine, I thought. My brother buried himself in studies, and my mom started dating. The dating thing was strange for me, but it was not something I couldn't run from, so I did. *My family was broken and so damaged it would not ever be fixed,* I thought to myself. All there was to do was eke out of it some sort of new life.

My best friend Ami's dad had told me that he would step in and be a father to me now, but only two months later, he was diagnosed with cancer as well and passed away before we graduated. It was a lonely time, but Ami and I found a fantastic way to run away . . . alcohol. We spent a good part of the last few years of high school drinking and partying. It was "fun"—well, more fun than dealing with our actual lives, anyhow, and we had each other, so that was awesome.

Most of the teachers had all but given up on me, and I couldn't care any less about school. It was fine with me because I had all but given up on school as well. Everyone but one, Coach Ketron, my weight-lifting coach. He also allowed me to help manage the football team, of which he was the head coach. Ketron watched me from a healthy distance, far enough away that I could live my grief out, but close enough that I was not able to do anything too stupid. I watched his kids every day after school during the football off-season. I am sure it was to keep an eye on me.

I found much joy in football and weight lifting. It was another way to wear myself out to the point that the rage and sadness in me would not run me ragged. It was fun; we even won state, and I had a bunch of big brothers whom I loved a lot. Looking back, I remember very few specifics or events in this period of life. It was like my brain just blacked out for a couple of years.

We had moved into a house in Larkspur at this point. It was far too painful to stay in the house of memories and hardship. Our new house was so peaceful, such a great place of sanctuary. It was there that I could feel God begin to heal my heart. I would sit on the big porch and watch the deer, who had twin fawns every year in the back pasture. She would walk out of the safety of the pasture right in front of me and eat with her little fawns. Such a proud momma she was. I had finally found a place I didn't want to run away from. My dogs, Earl and Sidney, were there as well to lay their big, fuzzy heads on my leg and tell me, "It's okay," when I didn't know if it was. I loved it there.

Around this time, I was starting to have issues with my health. I was always feeling sick or tired. My doctor had run some blood work because I had bronchitis I just could not kick. All my kidney values were off, and it appeared there was something very wrong with me. I was referred to a kidney specialist, who was concerned I might have leukemia. Fortunately, after many studies, it was shown that I had no cancer, but I had been pushing my body so hard in running and weight lifting that my body began to discard all the protein in my system. My muscles could no longer rebuild themselves, so I had to stop all athletic activity for a few months. I did not like that, but thank goodness, it was not cancer again. I'd already had enough of that in life. The doctor did say that with my kidneys as damaged as they were, it might be quite difficult to get and/or keep a pregnancy. That was not necessarily a huge problem at that point in my life. I figured I would just deal with that later.

One day, while hanging out with a few of the more country-type kids from school, I met this new guy. I didn't think much of it at first, but he was charming, quick-witted, funny, and a rascal—a pretty cute rascal at that. He was a bull-rider, cowboy type, and I soon found myself falling for him. I had always been partial to cowboy hats.

The new love I had in my life was all-encompassing. There was not a piece of my life that was not focused on going into the future with him. It was a connection that I needed so badly in my life with my father now gone, and he seemed to need me as much as I needed him. We were like fire and gasoline; every interest we shared and all the trouble we could get into, we did. We were soon engaged, just a few weeks before senior prom. *Finally*, I thought, *life had some excitement and hope to it.*

He introduced me to the rodeo community as a whole, and I fell in love with the community about as quickly as I fell for him. It was like having a big extended family that always had your back and would help you however you needed. There were about eight of these rough-stock event boys who were close, and I fit right in with them.

One family we were especially close to was the Browns. They had six kids: two of their own biological boys and four who had been adopted from the foster care system. I always thought it was so amazing that people would open their homes and hearts to kids in need. I dreamed maybe one day I would like to do that as well. We were no different; that family treated us the very same as all their kids, just one of the crew.

It was soon time to start looking into colleges. The Browns took us with them to tour multiple schools with rodeo programs, as their oldest son would be graduating as well. We were soon offered full-ride scholarships to attend a small college in southern Oklahoma. I was given a scholarship to manage the rodeo team, and my fiancé was given one to ride bulls for the college. It worked out so perfectly, we thought.

Now we could get out of Colorado and start a new, fresh life. After graduation, that is exactly what we did. We loaded up the dogs and all our stuff, and off to Oklahoma we went.

The college we attended did not provide very many dorm options, so we ended up renting a small house in town. It was a cute little place for a first home; the culture, however, was quite different from anything I had ever experienced. The police shut down the streets around us after dark to cut down on drive-by shootings. It was a town with a major drug and crime issue, which came as a surprise to me because it seemed so safe and the people were very nice.

I took a job at a veterinary practice, and my fiancé worked at a local restaurant. Our rodeo team was a mix of local kids from Texas and Oklahoma and a bunch of kids from Canada. I had never met anyone who could drink quite like they could. We hardly had any money to speak of, but we were having fun! With the famed college experience, we had every opportunity to party and do anything we wanted, really. We were free and young; what could go wrong?

We were living our "best life" when everything came careening to a halt with two little pink lines. It was a cold December day when, after quite a few days of feeling strange and missing a period, I decided to take a test. It was positive; I was pregnant! My fiancé was there with me when I found out, and we were both kind of scared.

What to do now? I knew the "options," and many people went over them with me many times, but I had already fallen in love with this tiny person. I quit the drinking, partying, and chewing cold turkey that day. My life now had so much more depending on it than just me.

Though I was excited, there were no celebrations for teenagers who found themselves pregnant. Some people made it very known that you were a disappointment and should be ashamed of yourself. Others smiled at you with a look of pity and fear behind their eyes. Celebration and congratulations were never ever the reaction.

I went to the health department to get some state insurance because that was my only option at that point. The appointments began soon thereafter, and we needed to do an ultrasound to see how far along I was exactly. When I looked at the screen, I saw a little, tiny Gummy Bear–looking baby with his heart beating away. I was overcome with joy to be a mother. They ran many tests and did all the routine prenatal care.

One day when I went in for a visit, the doctor explained to me that one of the genetic tests I had showed that my baby possibly had some issues and that I needed to go to Oklahoma City for more definitive tests. Oklahoma City was about three hours away, and I did not know how I was going to get the gas money to go all the way there. We could always opt to terminate the pregnancy if we could not go get the tests, I was reminded by the doctor—just as I was reminded almost every single visit. There was no way, I thought. We would find the money and go get our baby checked.

We pulled into the big car garage in Oklahoma City just a few weeks later. They checked us in and put us in a little room with so many books about genetic diseases in infants and paperwork. It looked more like an office for a professor or something. The specialist sat down with pictures in hand to explain to me that my baby had a rare genetic disorder, would possibly not be viable outside the womb, and that it might be best to go ahead and terminate the pregnancy. My heart was crushed, and all I could think was that I had seen my baby in ultrasounds, and he sure did not look like the babies in the pictures this doctor was showing me. I knew myself well enough to know termination was not an option. I could never live with myself after. I also knew after dealing with so many of my dad's doctors that they were only practicing medicine anyway.

"I want another option," I told them. "I want to keep my baby."

In order to do that, I would have to come back every few weeks to Oklahoma City for a special ultrasound. We barely had the money to make it to this first appointment, but that was just what we would have to do to keep our boy. It seemed as if no matter which doctor I saw, the best suggestion they would give a teenager like me was to terminate my baby. It was almost as if I was a bothersome addition to their docket that they would rather just get rid of instead of treat.

On a hot day in late August, my firstborn made his appearance into the world, perfectly formed and healthy. I was completely in love at first sight. The labor was very difficult. Because I had reached forty-two weeks of pregnancy, I went in on a Monday for an induction. Again, I felt as though I was some sort of annoyance for being there at all; everyone else in the labor department was held at a higher priority than I was, it felt like. The nurse would come in, turn the medication on, and I would have very strong contractions. Almost as soon as I felt I was in some sort of pattern, they would come in and turn the medication off in order to help another patient. It went on and on like this for forty-seven hours. That's when my doctor, who was not fluent in English, came in to tell me, "Baby no good. We have to take out now!"

I was beyond terrified. I understood that my baby was struggling, and it was time to have a C-section, but I had no idea what to expect or if he would even make it. I got into the operating room very quickly, and in what seemed like no time at all, a chunky little face was held over a blue cover in front of me. That was my boy, my whole heart, my Kash. In that moment, all the fight was worth it. My life was completely changed and, in many ways, saved, seeing that little guy who needed me.

Over the next few weeks, a nurse would come by the house every few days to check on me, my baby, and his development. Another "perk" of being a very young mom was that people would need to monitor how you did with your baby and make sure it was all up to their standards. I always had an underlying fear that one day the nurse would decide I was not doing as well as I should with my boy and take him away from me. The worst part was that I had no idea what I was doing at all, so how would I know what was expected of me anyway?

One morning I got up with my son, and I noticed what appeared to be blood on his shirt. Thinking he must have had a bloody nose or something, I proceeded to get him changed for the day. When I went to change his diaper, however, it had quite a bit of blood in it as well. My heart sank, and I was terrified. I got into the car right away and drove him to his pediatrician's office. Shaking from fear, I explained the situation, and we were immediately taken to the hospital for further tests.

Upon arrival at the hospital, a nurse came and got my son and asked me to wait in a separate room, of which I was not a fan. But she explained that she had to take Kash into the X-ray room and do a barium study to see what was wrong, and I was not allowed in the room due to radiation. However, I was soon joined in the room by a caseworker from the state. She began to ask me so many questions.

"What happened to your baby? Did you get mad at him? Did your fiancé get mad at him? Did you hit your baby on accident, maybe?"

"*No!*" I continuously said to her. "I swear, I would never hurt him!"

I was beyond terrified at that point, just begging them to bring my baby back or tell me where he was. It was a moment of so much fear that I could barely breathe. Just in time, the pediatrician came into the room.

"What the heck is going on in here? Why are you accusing her of such things with no proof?" He then proceeded to explain to me that my baby was not hurt at all; he had a milk allergy.

As soon as I heard that, I was so relieved by my vindication.

"Can I have my baby back now?" I asked him.

"Absolutely! Bring that baby in here immediately," he answered.

I held my baby like I had never held him before. *I was never letting him go again,* I thought to myself.

Kash recovered quickly, as I cut dairy completely out of my diet. Everything calmed down, and I had a sneaking suspicion for some reason that God had stepped in at the hospital to not allow my son to be taken from me. It seemed ridiculous. For years, I had only thought of God long enough to blame Him for not healing my dad and causing his death. Still, though, I knew something had been there for me, vindicating me and returning my son to my arms.

Maybe I should start back into the church, I thought to myself. *I am a mother now, after all.*

My fiancé and I tried a few churches here and there, but nothing really clicked. We were living together unmarried, after all, and that was frowned upon for obvious reasons. The other feeling that kept creeping up on me was the longing to go back home to Colorado, where my family was, to help me with my new little guy. Soon that was just what we did. We moved back home to Colorado, and we also fixed that being unmarried issue in a small family ceremony. We were happy to be home in Colorado and married with our new baby; it was a cute picture for sure.

We moved up to northern Colorado for a job my new husband had acquired, and there was an awesome church we found. They were like no church family I had ever met before; they loved us a lot! I reconnected there with a friend whom I had known in the rodeo community from high school, and she became closer to a sister to me than any other relationship I had ever had. I absolutely loved my life and the growth we were experiencing. Even better, we found out we were pregnant again, this time with a baby girl. I was so beyond excited about the addition to our little family, and believe it or not, people were happy for us this time! My doctor's office even gave me a congratulatory gift basket.

Wow, I thought. *Is this what it's like for most people to have a new baby on the way?*

It was all going well until one day my husband turned to me and said, "I want a divorce."

Wait, what? I must have heard that wrong. Yes, we had some struggles as any young couple did, but a divorce? Surely not! Unfortunately, it was true. My marriage was over, just over, that quickly. I remember sitting in my truck, looking down at my pregnant belly and then at my sleeping son in his car seat in the back.

What now? I knew I could go back to Larkspur with my mom and my old life, but that was not going to be a healthy life choice. I knew the choices I would go right back to making. It was a Tuesday night though, and the church was having a service that night. I was not sure what they would do to help me, but I did know I was not going to be headed back home. Home was gone for all three of us.

Chapter Three

AS I WALKED into church that evening, I had no idea what to do or say or even whom to say it to. The youth pastor, Greg, and his wife, Tracey, noticed that something was wrong with me. I explained the situation and that I had nowhere to go and really no money to my name. They put some money in my hand and gave me a room big enough for me and my son, but after the baby came, we would need to find a bigger place. I thought, well, this would probably be a temporary deal anyway because I figured I would be headed home in no time.

That was not the case, however. Another couple helped to take all my dogs, cat, and horses to their house, and slowly but surely, all my stuff was stored somewhere. The youth pastor's house was a very safe and calm place to be. It had a big apple tree on the front lawn, which Kash called his happy tree. Somehow that little boy was strong and resilient through all the hardship that we found ourselves in.

After looking around for a few weeks, I met another couple at church who offered me a basement apartment to stay in. It was big enough for me and both of my babies to stay in, at least until I could get my feet on the ground again. The only problem was that the owners of this house basically had a museum of priceless cowboy artifacts in this basement. My eyes were huge with concern, watching my now-two-year-old running wild through all this beautiful stuff.

"Not to worry," they said. "He can't really hurt anything down here."

I was not as convinced, but we decided to move in, and it was truly a perfect home for us in that season. Not only did we have space and were surrounded by beautiful things, but we found a family with these people. It was very much like having a dad again. I was constantly included in every aspect of life in that house. It was so healing for my heart in many ways.

The winter wind blew cold, and I again found myself a few weeks past my due date and headed in for my induction. I had not told my doctor about all the personal drama I had in my life for fear I would get to hear about all my "options" again. The delivery room was pretty tense. My husband showed up for the birth of our daughter, but so did my newfound family in the church. I just told myself I needed to focus on having this baby and keeping myself calm.

At ten that evening, I started pushing and was successfully able to deliver my daughter naturally. She was beautiful and instantly captured my heart the same way her brother had just a few years before. Tyelee Maysen—what a beautiful blessing amid so much pain. The Browns came to hang out with Kash while I delivered his new baby sister. Never was there a prouder brother when he was able to come see her. He sat up so proudly and held her.

I thought to myself, *This is all worth it, worth every bit of it. My kids are the best.*

Soon thereafter, I knew it was time to try to get out on my own. The family I was living with was so sad to see us go though. They would have kept us forever if they could have. I found a nice little house with some acreage for my horses and enough room to get my dogs and cat back. It was one thousand dollars a month for rent, which was pretty steep for someone with no job or money. However, I felt like this was the place we needed to be, and I was going to trust God to be my provider.

We moved in, and I began job hunting. I found a job at a veterinary practice. I secured some day care and started busting my butt for my little family. It went well. I loved the people I worked with. They always took care of me and were very understanding and flexible with my situation.

The season was difficult, but seemed to be going as well as could be expected. I was so excited to have my dogs back. At this point, I had four: Earl, Rio, Ace, and Dollar. Sidney had stayed with my mom when I went to college because my mom was pretty attached to her, and she did better not moving here and there. After getting Earl back, however, I noticed he was not the big muscle-bound dog I had once had. He kept losing weight, and nothing seemed to help him out.

Luckily, I worked at a veterinary practice, which ran every test in the book on him. It turned out that he had a muscle-wasting disease, and there was no cure. I saw he was suffering and one day took him to work with me, knowing it was time for him to go to heaven. I sat and held his paw as he passed away. It was a tragic loss, one of the most tragic I had ever experienced. This dog had been with me through so much of life and had comforted me more than anything else in every hard moment. The strange thing was that I could not even shed a tear at his passing. I just got up and went back to work for the day. I could not afford to take the day off.

As I walked away from him, I said to myself, *There is something truly wrong with me. How can I just walk away and not be completely destroyed in this moment?* It was like an out-of-body experience, and I was dead inside. A large part of me was completely unresponsive.

Life went on, and I continued working and being a mom to the best of my ability. My divorce had been finalized that March, and many people were ready and eager for me to move on with my life, much more so than I was. I had been growing so much in my faith. The Lord was dealing with me on so many things in life. I knew if I was going to move on with life and find a new man, I would definitely want it to be God's best for me.

I wrote a list of all the qualities I wanted in a godly man to raise my family with. Everything I wanted in a man, I was finding, actually matched the personality and character of God Himself, and I was willing to wait for the right guy. I spent most of my time with the church family I had now, especially one older lady named Jane.

She was the first prophetic person I had ever really met in my life. She could tell me so many things about myself. Jane told me so many stories about her life and walk with God. It inspired me so much. I wanted to be just like her when I grew up, I thought to myself. She was in her eighties by then, and when her nurses would come to help her at her house, she would tell them how she was planning to go homestead in Alaska. Alaska Jane, they called her. She was my spiritual mentor, but not only that, she was one of my very best friends.

One day I answered a call from my best friend (and basically my sister) Kirste. She stated that she had been at the rodeo earlier that weekend and a certain guy there had said to her how absolutely gorgeous he found me and that he would like my phone number. Nic Ford was his name. I had known him from the rodeo community and had even had dinner with him and his brother once a few years before, but I had not thought much of it.

"How would he even remember me, Kirst?" I said in disbelief.

"He saw you at church a few weeks ago and heard you are now single," she explained.

Just a Life Story

"I guess he can give me a call," I said, and her plot thickened.

Without my knowledge, Kirste had decided to try her hand at matchmaking. She then took that open door to Nic. "I know a girl who super-likes you and asked me to give you her number," she explained to a very surprised man. "It's Kaity; she thinks you're very cute."

He must have been somewhat interested in her proposition because the texts started coming in.

After a few weeks of texting back and forth, it became apparent that this guy was going to dance around asking me on a date until Jesus came back; therefore, it would be left up to me to get this ball rolling. After explaining that Kash was going to be competing in a mutton-busting event coming up soon, I played the damsel-in-distress role as well as any human could and asked, "Can you please help me get him some rodeo gear? I have no idea what to buy at all."

He replied, "Oh, absolutely. I know what he will need."

What a sucker, I thought to myself proudly.

Later that week, we met at a feedstore that had some rodeo stuff for little kids. As he walked into the store, I noticed his handsome blue eyes under his black cowboy hat. He was also very tall, tall enough I could wear my high heels and easily be shorter than him. I was very impressed with Kirste's idea so far. "Well done, sister," I said under my breath.

We looked around for a bit there but just could not find anything suitable for my little cowboy. We had to go to some other stores, and this adventure had to continue. As we were driving to the next location, the driver next to me gave me the "roll down your window" hand gesture.

"You have a flat tire!" they yelled through the traffic.

I waved thank you to them, and off to the tire place we went. While waiting for my tire to be fixed, my kids were climbing all over Nic. I figured this was a good example of what life was like with us. He would have to get used to this if he was going to stick around; might as well break him in early.

A lady who was also waiting for her tire to be fixed looked over at Nic and with a big smile said, "Your kids are beautiful."

I held my breath; the moment of truth had arrived. How would he respond?

A large smile spread across his face, and he replied, "Well, thank you so much." He smiled from across the room and gave me a joking kind of wink, Kash on his shoulders and Tyelee hanging off his leg.

My shopping days were over. *SOLD! I'll take the cowboy in the black hat!*

From that point forward, things rolled on very quickly. We were engaged no more than seven months later and married four months after that. On a warm July day, I became Kaitlin Rene Ford, and that would prove to be one of the best things I could have ever been.

We moved onto his family's property into a small white farmhouse. It was a quaint, wonderful home with my in-laws just about two hundred yards down the lane. My kids had found a wonderful country life, with many people who adored them in every sense of the word. The only thing about this new place was that it was a bit behind in centuries. What I mean by that is, there was only a woodburning stove in the whole house. As a girl from Douglas County, I was much more accustomed to thermostats and heat.

"There is no need for that; people have used wood to heat themselves for years," my father-in-law explained.

Determined to be the best possible new wife, I was going to give it my best try. Only one issue—I had no idea how to light a fire. My sweet husband showed me how it worked, and I finally got it lit. However, there was one other issue: acrylic nails are flammable, it turns out. Yes, I set my thumbnail on fire directly. I was personally warmer, but my house was not. This was not going to last long, and soon men came to put a furnace in my new home.

Chapter Four

I ENJOYED BEING married. The man the Lord had brought into my life was exactly what I had prayed for. Everything I had written on that list of what I wanted in a husband, he was. As good love goes, it was only a few months into our marriage before I started feeling that old familiar feeling. I knew I was pregnant again. It was a time of celebration and excitement. Nic was such a proud papa already.

I was still working at the vet's office at this time, and one day at work, I started bleeding. It was terrifying. I wanted my baby! I went to the doctor, and he confirmed I was indeed pregnant and, after running some tests, determined there was a baby and that the baby was still alive. However, the doctor said that I had most likely been pregnant with twins and lost one, but there was no way to prove that was the case or the reason for the bleeding. I was left in a strange place, grieving a child I was not sure was lost but grateful for the one I still had growing in me. We went on believing that no matter what, God was in control of the situation. If our baby had gone back to heaven, then God would be holding him, and that was a safe place.

Life went on, and my pregnancy progressed, and by that winter, I was already starting to show. My new marriage was wonderful. It was a definite feeling of a redemptive season, until one day I picked up my new husband's phone and noticed the internet browser was open to a porn site. *Devastated* was not even the word for it. I felt I had found a promised land that had lies deep within it. I confronted Nic about what I had found and told him I was not planning on having a marriage like my parents', where I was not his one and only love. He agreed, repented to me, and got some accountability partners in the church to help him with this addiction.

Addiction was exactly what it was. I understood it well. I had been not only a workout addict—to the point that I almost destroyed my kidneys—but also an alcoholic, a chewer, and had even dealt with porn addiction of my own. I knew how difficult it was to get free.

I quit, and so will he, I thought to myself. *We have so much life to live, and I do love him, so we will make this work.*

On a hot July day, being about forty-two weeks pregnant, I again went to the doctor for my check-up.

"You're in labor," he said, and off to the hospital I went.

About thirteen hours later, I held my beautiful new daughter. I wanted to name her after someone amazing, and therefore, Laska Jane seemed very fitting. Also, Nic's mom, who is a wonderful lady, is named Jane, so it fit her perfectly. What a beautiful gift we had been given! Is there anything better?

My son, who desperately wanted a brother, instantly fell in love with his new sister and was as proud and excited to hold and welcome her as he was his first sister. Tyelee was over the moon about her new sister, and what a bond they developed even at such a young age. It was a beautiful time in life, and it got increasingly more beautiful when, just two years later, we welcomed another daughter into our lives. Wacey Rose was born on another hot day in July and quickly became the apple of our eye as well as her brother's. She had more fire and sass than anyone I had met in my life, though she was so petite in stature. Life was great! The Lord blessed us abundantly.

We were still attending the cowboy church, and I had started serving on the prayer team. I was new to the whole idea of praying for others and was a bit nervous about what exactly I would say anyway. Our group leaders began teaching us through an inner healing prayer model, and boy, did I need it. This new way of prayer and hearing truth from God was delivering me from years and years of pain. From my dad's death, to Earl, to my divorce, I learned that God had a whole lot to say about almost everything in my life. I had been to many counseling sessions in my life, but this was far more effective in so much less time. I began to study spiritual warfare and came to the knowledge of a real yet defeated enemy. So much of my life began to make sense, and I felt a deeper call was about to come forth over our lives.

Nic had gone up hunting that year, and I was home with the kids one day when, clear as a bell, I heard the Lord speak to me. "I want you to do foster care and adopt children."

No way, buddy, I thought. *There is no way in heck I could take children into my home and then send them back to their families, and also, how would I ever adopt anyone and love them like my children?* I laughed to myself. *That would not be a good life for them. I am a good mom, but not like that kind of mom.*

It all seemed too ridiculous to even imagine, but it was ringing in my ears repeatedly, driving me crazy. I knew it was the voice of the Lord, calling on my life. However, there was no possible way I could do that.

I told the Lord, "Yes, I heard you call, and yes, I will follow you, but you need to first confirm this word with my husband."

Now that's that, I thought. I had gotten myself out of it by using the good old "head of the household" rule. Nic would never go for something like this because our hands were already full anyway.

That next day, when my husband came home from hunting, he said, "Honey, I have something I need to talk with you about. I feel the Lord is calling us into foster care and possibly adoption."

You could have knocked me over with a feather! That sneaky God of the universe had done exactly what I had asked!

Well, that settled it. We were called and were going, whether I thought it was a good idea or not.

Nic decided that since that was our new calling, it was time for him to get a vasectomy—so that we could ensure space in our lives for other kids. The doctor who had told me that it would be very difficult for me to get and sustain a pregnancy had so far not been very accurate, and it would be just a matter of time before I was pregnant again. I, however, hated this idea with the passion of one billion burning suns. I was not done being pregnant! I wanted to have more babies, but my husband was so sure this was the right decision. The day we went in for his procedure, the nurse came to call him into the surgery room, and my husband turned to me as white as a sheet, with pure terror in his eyes.

I looked back at him and said, "You go in there! You chose this!"

That poor nurse looked at me like I was some sort of nutcase as she pried Nic's hand off mine and walked him to his fate. Secretly, in the most rebellious way, I prayed in the waiting room that not only would it hurt a little but that it would not work at all. Well, it did work, and I mourned my dream of being pregnant again for weeks. Until one day, the Lord got a hold of me and let me know that, first of all, my husband was right and my attitude was unacceptable. Secondly, being that He is a very big God, I needed to trust Him to hold my dreams as well.

I finally found peace in going on with our new calling, and we began to figure out the steps to take to become foster parents. We had to get training, figure out if we wanted to use an agency or not, and about one thousand other things.

One of the biggest things we needed to get done was to make room in our house. We thought about moving to a bigger house, but we didn't want to leave our portion of the family property. So we had a great idea! We would just rebuild our whole house. We would put an addition on the upstairs of our house, taking our house down to the studs and completely redoing the entire floor plan. We found a builder and came up with a plan to go from a four-bedroom, one-bathroom house to a six-bedroom, three-and-a-half-bathroom house. In the meantime, we would get a camper, put it in the pasture, and live in that with our four kids. It would only be six months anyway, so what could go wrong?

Turns out a whole lot of things can go wrong when you build a house, especially when you live in a camper in a pasture.

A dear couple from the church had given us a fifth-wheel camper to stay in while our house was being built, and we were so thankful. What a fun adventure it would be! However, by day three of having to set the table and couch back up after the kids got up from using them as beds, I was already a bit over it. We bought a large freight box to store all our stuff in during the rebuild and only took the bare minimum into the camper. That being said, with six people in a camper, it was pretty stuffed. It was July when we moved into the camper, so the kids spent a good part of their days outside playing, which helped.

Everything seemed to be going smoothly with the build, until our builder had a heart attack. He was fine but needed a few weeks to recover. Obviously, we were okay with that, and a few weeks later, they started building again. Meanwhile, we were figuring out all the extra adventures that went along with camper life. We had no hot water in the camper, so we had to all shower at my in-laws' house. There were so many people that we had to get on a shower schedule. I got the Tuesday and Friday shower schedule. I am sure I was a joy to sit by when Sunday rolled around.

We also had to go into town to use the laundromat to clean all our clothes. I met many interesting friends there, including one sweet man with two twin girls. Their names were Mary and Jane—not because of weed, he explained, but because they rhymed.

One November morning, I awoke to find it was the first snow of the year. What a beautiful thought, except the first snow I woke up to was in my bed—my literal bed. There was snow on me, my whole bed, and all my clothes. So we had to pull the slide-out back in, which made our small area much smaller. The fun just kept coming.

Then one day a sweet young man working on our house destroyed our main power line and pulled the power box off the house; luckily, he was fine. It would not have been an issue at all except that it was the power to the camper as well, and it was January.

After a week of staying at my in-laws', the power went back on, but everything in the camper had frozen. It had been so cold that the refrigerator froze. Then the water spigot we had been using to fill the camper's water containers froze as well. To get water, we had to stretch a hose to my brother-in-law's spigot, which was about three hundred yards from the camper, and then walk the hose line to make sure it did not freeze. I got my steps in every other day, getting water for my family. I also had to handwash every single thing we ate off or cooked with in freezing water every day.

Needless to say, it was not going as amazingly as we thought it would, but that was not even the worst of it. The worst was the fact that we had decided to try and run a sewer line from the camper to the old septic tank, which had seemed to be going just fine until it also froze. Nic had to use a large stick and shove whatever had happened in the toilet that day down as far as possible and then flush that down with a large amount of water, and that seemed to take it down.

I felt like I was at the end of my rope and I could not take any more hits when, yet again, that pesky little porn problem of Nic's decided to return. I was hurt, yes. At this point, I was more ticked off that the enemy was still trying to take my husband down with this sin. So, through the pain of it all, I decided, as his wife, to use all my inner healing prayer knowledge to help my husband get free from this thing that haunted him. We worked through all the years of rejections and shame that this addiction was rooted in and got rid of it for good! When I understood that this had very little to do with me and much more to do with the fact that the enemy was attacking my husband, I decided to rise up and fight by his side against it. And we won—he got free!

The building was going slowly, very slowly, but steadily. We were into spring, and our house was finally taking form. On one trip back from our wonderful watering hole, Nic threw his back out. The only option was to throw him over my shoulder and hoist him in and out of the camper for the next couple of days. It took all my strength to lift him, but after just a few days, he was feeling better. If that was not enough to deal with, I had decided to try to go on the keto diet a couple of weeks before, and I woke up on a May morning with a terrible pain in my stomach. I had had kidney stones in the past, and it felt like that, but in the front of my stomach. We went to the emergency room, and the doctor explained to me that I needed surgery.

Surely not, I thought. I would go home, and it would work itself out. Eight days later, I was in emergency surgery to have my gallbladder removed. My keto diet had been a success. I lost the equivalent of the weight of a gallbladder.

That same week, our builder informed us that he had underbid our project to the tune of about one hundred thousand dollars and needed that money immediately to finish the project. We did not feel comfortable giving him any more money. He basically said that we could finish the rest of the building ourselves and pay for the subcontractors because he would not be returning. We had thirty days to finish the house to get an appraisal and get the extra money to pay everyone. I figured we had just spent a year in a camper for no reason at all because there would be no way we could even pay a loan with an extra hundred thousand dollars on it, and we would end up having to sell our new house.

Our wonderful church family came to our assistance and helped us with all the finishing work in the house, and my father-in-law painted it inside and out. As the final gut punch of the season, I woke up one morning, exhausted from working on the house, and noticed a large lump on the side of my neck.

A goiter! That's all I need, I thought. But luckily, it was just a locked muscle from being unable to put my arm down for the eight days I sat not wanting surgery for my gallbladder. Fortunately, I was doing so much painting it worked itself out without physical therapy!

The Lord made a way and saved our butts financially. We moved into our beautiful new home on my husband's birthday, June 27, almost an entire year since we had started on this grand adventure.

Chapter Five

AFTER TAKING SOME recovery time from building the house, it was time to start training for foster care. We decided to do training through a Christian company that got all your certifications and helped you find an agency or human services department to work through. It was an eye-opening experience to learn about the heart of God for all these kids in need. One of the other aspects of this training was making sure the community around the foster family and future foster children was well structured and supportive; it does take a village, after all.

As always, our church family went above and beyond to come beside us and attend training to be the very best community to bring these sweet babies into. We decided to go with an agency to help facilitate our fostering; this provided foster families with an advocate and further support system. Training took about six months to complete, and finally, we were certified! I figured the calls would be pouring in the very next week, if not the very next day, so I waited expectantly.

The call finally came in about six weeks later!

Just a Life Story

"We have a little girl in need of emergency immediate placement. Are you ready?" asked our amazing caseworker.

I had waited so long, and the moment was here, but the nerves were definitely there as well. I had prayed about it for so long, and I know the Lord had told me, "You say yes, and I'll do the rest." So *yes* was the answer.

I drove down to the Target parking lot in the snow and cold. I pulled up next to a Ford Explorer, and a caseworker from Denver County stepped out. She was a nice-enough lady, greeting me with a tired smile and opening the back door. There she was—the reason we had worked so hard and done so much in the last year. Her beautiful brown eyes looked up at me, and I could see fear in them. That took me a little off guard. One of the best days of my life was one of her worst.

"Hi, baby, it's okay; you're safe now," I said to her.

The caseworker took her out of her car seat and handed her to me.

"What does she like to eat? Does she have any allergies? What size clothes does she wear? Is there anything I need to know about her?" I asked.

"I have no idea," said the caseworker. "There is no real information I can give you."

She arrived with nothing except a premade backpack from the Social Services Department. So, with no information and no real personal belongings, I headed home from a Target parking lot with a person who did not know or trust me at all. This was not exactly what I thought it would be like. Not that I thought it would be glamourous, but this had not even a hint of glamour at all, not even close. I wondered if she had a favorite toy or blanket or something. Was there anything at all that had brought her joy or comfort in her young life that now was lost and left behind? There was no way to know, and that broke me. She was safe now though. Whether she knew it yet or not, she was safe with me.

Upon walking through the door with this beautiful gift, there were four small people and a daddy waiting eagerly. The moment we walked in, they all fell in love with this baby. She was a bit apprehensive and just wanted to find a place of quiet to decompress from all that had transpired that day and probably her whole life. The place she found was with our yellow Labrador, Rio.

Rio had been rescued a few years earlier from a breeding kennel that had been too rough in training for such a sensitive dog. Rio was scared of everything and everyone when we first picked her up, and she would try to run away every single day. But I would chase her down and bring her home every time. Eventually, she knew that we were safe and also that we were not letting her get away, so she might as well love us and stay. On this day, Rio got to show this scared little girl the same thing! She was safe, and we were not going to let her go.

Soon that scared little girl was a wild, happy rascal running through my house with her sisters and brother. She fit in wonderfully in our home, like she had always been there. The foster process was running its course, and I got to meet her mother. She was a sweet lady who loved her daughter, but she knew she could not provide a safe place for this baby to grow up. Her mother grew to love and trust that her baby was safer with me. After she had made that decision, she kind of just disappeared.

The caseworker explained that at this point, it looked as if we would be headed into an adoptive situation, and we needed to decide whether we were willing to be a permanent family option. We held a family vote, and it was a unanimous and resounding *yes*! She was going to be with us forever! We hoped and prepared our home, life, and hearts to live the rest of our days with another daughter and sister.

However, about a month later, the DNA profile that the county ran to confirm paternity came back with a result. The father we thought was her dad turned out to be not her real father. Her real father came into the picture, and he and his family wanted a relationship with our baby girl. We began visits with this side of her family and eventually met her aunt, who was willing to take and raise her as her own daughter.

I honestly wanted to fight it and keep my baby, but her aunt was wonderful! The biological family always gets first consideration in the system, and in this case, it was clear that this was a great placement. *Crushed* does not even begin to describe the feeling I felt knowing that the baby we fell in love with and were planning to have forever was now moving into her forever home without us. Her aunt promised we could stay in her life, but I knew that would be completely up to her because we had no right to stay in her life.

I called our caseworker through the agency and explained to her that our entire family was absolutely devastated that we were not going to be this beautiful girl's forever family. We were so excited for her to have a safe place to go back to in her biological family, but maybe we were just not cut out for this sort of thing because it was too painful. My little kids were just not okay. They had given so much, from their home to their hearts. They had given it all and were now devastated.

We still had a heart for adoption and had come all this way to answer the call. All we could do was pray that God would make a way. The caseworker thought for a bit and called me back a few days later with a new idea for us: embryo adoption.

Embryo adoption? What the heck is that? I thought.

She explained that embryo adoption occurs when a family who has gone through the in vitro fertilization process can, for some reason, not use all their embryos. Believing that life begins at fertilization, we knew these were babies who needed an adoptive family to give them life. These families have only four options when they have embryos that they cannot use. Those options are to keep them frozen forever, donate them to science, destroy them, or put them out up adoption. My mind was boggled!

"So could I give birth to my own adopted children?" I asked.

"Yes." She went on to explain that these babies don't get adopted as often because most people looking to adopt are unable to have children... but I was able to.

As shocked as I was, I felt the peace of God resting upon this and knew I had to talk to Nic about it.

After a long but basic description of what I had just learned, I retold it all to Nic.

Immediately he said, "Yes, let's do it."

Seriously? I thought. *Just like that, "let's do it"?*

"Yes," he said, "I feel like this is what God has for us to do next."

We went forward with the process and somehow paid all the adoption fees rather quickly. Soon our adoption profile had gone live and was sent to all the potential families for review and consideration. Only a week or so later, I got a call from the adoption agency that our profile had been selected by a family. I felt like the confirmation that these were our babies would be that they were from one of the Carolinas. Why that was, I am not sure. I just felt like the Lord told me that was how I would know for sure.

The phone rang one day in October. "Your profile has been selected," the adoption specialist explained. "We have six embryos for you!"

Six? Oh my goodness, that is way too many, I thought. But my mouth said, "Oh, I see, well, we will have to clear them with our clinic and make sure they would be a good blood type match," figuring my clinic would get me out of it.

"Already done," said the adoption lady. "They have accepted the embryos, and they are compatible with your blood type!"

Oh boy! Now how am I going to say no without saying no?

"Well, we will have to figure out shipping, and I am not even sure where these embryos are from anyway," I explained, still looking for a good reason to get out of it.

"They are from South Carolina," she said.

I could hear Nic laughing from the other room, and it seemed God was laughing a bit too.

"South freaking Carolina? Just like God said, huh?" I said under my breath.

"So, are we moving forward?" the voice on the other end of the line asked.

The words "You say yes, and I will do the rest" were ringing in my ears.

"*Yes,*" I said, "Let's do this."

We only had the final contracts to sign, and they would be drafted in the next few weeks.

Our foster daughter was still with us part-time at this point, as she was transitioning into life with her aunt. We loved her as much as we could on the days we had her and tried to heal on the days she was gone. My momma heart was still crushed but hopeful for the next season. I decided to go see a dear friend of mine, Stacie. She was always a place of healing for my heart during this time, just to get a break from all the ups and downs of this season. Nic had a cough, and the kids were still dealing with a lot, but Nic said he felt I definitely needed to go. While I was at church with Stacie that Sunday, a small lady named Rosey came up to me and put her hand on my belly.

She began to speak a prophetic word over me. "You know their names. Write their names," she practically yelled at me. "The Lord is going to do a great miracle for you this December."

I was very excited and encouraged by her words! I knew we actually did have six baby names, two girl names and four boy names. Stowick, Tekoa, Benaiah, Urijah, Mariah, and Mahalia. I wrote them all down as the vision statement for the next season.

Now, what was that miracle she spoke of? Would we actually get to keep our little foster daughter? Would I be pregnant that quickly with our embryos? I thought of so many things on my way home. When I got home, I knew we had only a few more days with my little girl before she would fully transition to her new home. We took some family pictures and then took her to her aunt's house, fully expecting to get her back sometime in the last two weeks of transition.

This year, however, was 2020, after all, and her aunt ended up with COVID. They were in quarantine for the last bit of transition, and our girl did not come back to our home. Adding insult to injury was what it was. It had already been so painful, but then the unexpected and sudden break was almost too much to bear. We were trying to catch our breath from that sudden blow when my dear Nic, who had still been coughing, woke up the next morning with a large lump on his neck.

"Kaity, can you come feel this?" he asked me.

I felt it, and immediately I knew this was very bad. I did not want to say anything incorrect, but I knew he needed to be checked out that day.

Nic went to the doctor by himself because COVID restrictions would not allow us to go in with him. They took a chest X-ray and saw a tumor about the size of a hot dog in his chest. My husband had cancer. He called to let me know the findings the doctor had made, and I told him with as much courage as I could muster, "You will live and not die; don't be afraid!"

After we hung up the phone, I collapsed on the floor. I was in so much emotional anguish, I could not even stand up. All the memories from the past came rushing back... the treatments and sickness and death. It was too much to bear. I called my pastors, who at this point in my life were much more spiritual parents than pastors. They prayed with me, and I heard God say clear as a bell: "Baby girl, you have to fight back!"

Fight back, I would. We still had to tell our kids. Somehow even after their sister went back home, they had another earth-shaking event coming down the pike at them. At the moment we were trying to explain the situation to my in-laws and the kids that Nic was very sick, my phone kept ringing and ringing. I had totally forgotten I was supposed to be in virtual court that day for the last foster placement hearing.

The mother of our foster daughter did not want the father's sister to take the baby and instead wanted to force the courts to allow us to adopt her daughter.

"Mrs. Ford, do you believe that the aunt of this child is a suitable placement for her?" one lawyer asked.

"Yes," I replied.

"Don't you love her? Don't you want to keep her?" the other lawyer argued.

"Of course we love her and want to keep her! However, I want her to have her biological family as well," I replied.

"Well, do you really know these people? How do you know she is safe?" she angrily asked.

"I don't know. I don't know," I said, now in tears.

"Is there a real reason that you can't keep this baby then? Do you just not want to?" she snapped back.

"Well, my husband was diagnosed with cancer this morning, and I don't know if I can continue even being a foster parent at this time," I said.

The virtual room fell silent, and my heart was completely shattered. There it was. I was losing my beautiful little girl because I couldn't do it all, and cancer was going to steal my everything again.

"That's enough!" said the judge. "Mrs. Ford, we are all sorry to hear that, and you are dismissed from these proceedings. Thank you for all you have done for this little girl." And the call ended.

Everyone was in court that day—from the caseworkers to the agency to the biological parents to the aunt—and they all knew now that we were in a bad way. My phone blew up with calls and well-wishes. I knew our embryo adoption was not in jeopardy, but at this moment, we had to get to Texas to get Nic treatment. Our foster daughter's aunt brought her for dinner before we were to leave for Texas so she could see us and Nic. We became her godparents that day, and at least we knew we would still be in her life forever, which was a huge blessing and relief. We were at the end of one battle and into another, and we were going to fight back with all we had.

Chapter Six

I FOUND THE TUMOR in his neck. I felt it with my own hand, just like my own mother and father did. It was almost unbelievable. The next few days were extremely hectic and stressful. It was becoming increasingly apparent that the disease in Nic's body was progressing extremely quickly. We went to our family doctor, and I asked for a referral to MD Anderson, Houston. I knew enough from my dad's sickness that this was the best place to go. They had the very best doctors and cutting-edge treatments. Also, I figured if we were going to fight back, we should do it with the biggest and best ammo we could find in heaven and on Earth.

Usually, you have to have a referral from an oncology office to get an appointment with the specialists in Houston, but ours was accepted. God had begun to lead us on the path. I called to get Nic an appointment, and they said the soonest they could get him in was December 12; that was still almost two weeks away. I was just praying he could last that long because he was already having trouble swallowing, and his chest cavity had begun to fill with fluid. Later that day, he was back in the emergency room, unable to breathe again. There was nothing they could do with that tumor in his chest. I knew we had to go to Texas now if we were going to go.

We had a small impromptu birthday party for my oldest daughter, Tyelee, because I knew we would not be back from Texas in time for her birthday. Nic made her birthday cake—because he makes all our kids' cakes every year. He could barely even sit long enough to decorate the cake without needing to lie back down to breathe.

By the next day, we were on a plane to Houston. I was so nervous that we would get up in the air and the pressure of flying plus the fluid in his chest would cause a huge emergency issue. I prayed the whole time under my mask, because on top of everything, it was still COVID season. We finally landed after what felt like hours and hours, and I grabbed all the bags, found a cab, and helped my usually big, strong husband with everything. He was so weak and could hardly do anything at all.

We arrived at the hotel for people attending the hospital, and we planned on waiting for his appointment if we possibly could, but knew there was an oncology emergency room if that was not possible. Two days later, we walked down the street to get something to eat, and I turned to look at Nic. He was pale white and could no longer keep up with me. I knew it was time for treatment. He was not ready; he was scared and did not want to go into the unknown of the hospital, but who would? We went back up to the room, and I told him he had to go in, which he protested until we realized he could hardly even swallow the water I had handed him.

Nic finally agreed to walk across the road to the emergency room. As we walked in, they placed Nic in a wheelchair, and it seemed the whole room was yelling at me.

"Ma'am, you cannot be in here! You have to go!" everyone yelled at me because of COVID.

"I have some numbers and information I need to tell the nurse, and I am not leaving until I do," I said firmly.

I am not sure if they had a panic button or what, but then an armed officer walked in and said, "Is there a problem, ma'am?"

Is there a problem? I am in an oncology emergency room with my thirty-seven-year-old husband; yes, there is a major problem, I thought to myself.

"No, sir, I just need to give the nurse some information and numbers, and I am not leaving until I do," I repeated. "I have my mask on, so that should be fine, right?"

"Ma'am, it's time to go," the officer said as he motioned toward the door.

"I am sorry, Officer Jimmy. You can arrest me if need be, but I need the nurse to know some things about my husband," I explained in all seriousness.

Seeing that I was not going to budge, Officer Jimmy said, "Can we get a nurse out here quickly?"

Finally, a nurse walked out, and I explained the information and brief history of what was going on with Nic.

"Thank you, ma'am. Now say goodbye," she said to me.

I turned to Nic and saw the fear in his eyes, but I knew this was the place he was supposed to be.

I kissed him and said, "I love you, and I will see you soon," and at that, they whisked him away into the back. I walked out the door with Officer Jimmy.

As I walked back across the road, the reality of my loneliness and helplessness set in. I cried all the way back to my room. When I got up to the room, I realized Nic's phone charger was sitting on the counter, and I knew his phone was about to die as we were walking into the ER.

Now what do I do? I knew I would most definitely be arrested by dear, sweet Officer Jimmy if I walked back over there. Luckily, I was able to give my information, including my phone number, to the nurse so that I could be contacted. I sat in the room in silence for a while, not knowing what was happening just across the road, yet a sense of peace and comfort entered the room. The peace that passes understanding was all it could have possibly been in this chaos.

After what seemed like forever, my phone rang, and it was the doctor from the emergency department.

"Mrs. Ford?" she said.

"Yes, that's me," I answered.

"Mrs. Ford," she continued, "I am not going to sugarcoat the situation your husband is in. We are attempting to confirm his diagnosis, but at this point, he is in full kidney failure;

the tumor in his chest has grown exponentially to about the size of a cantaloupe, and there is fluid all the way around his lungs. If he makes it through the night, we may have a shot at treatment, but that's a big *if* at this point."

I remained calm somehow and asked, "Well, did you tell him all of that?"

"I am headed in to tell him right now," she replied.

"Don't tell him the 'make it through the night' part; just tell him the basics, please. I don't want him to freak out," I requested.

"I will give him the information he needs, but I will not scare him. However, you need to understand the situation." Her voice was softer now. I am sure it is hard to tell people things like that.

"Thank you. What is he doing anyway? His phone is dead, and I am just wondering," I asked her.

"Well, he appears to be eating a sandwich and watching *Swamp People*," she said with a small chuckle.

"He is going to make it," I chuckled back.

We said our goodbyes, and I prepared for a long night of waiting on the Lord to intervene and hoped that in the morning I would hear my husband's voice again. The night was long, filled with prayer and listening to the song "Promises" by Maverick City Music. I would like to say that I had so much faith I slept like a baby, but really, I slept maybe one or two hours, max.

The next morning I got a call from an oncologist. He explained to me that Nic was officially diagnosed with acute lymphatic leukemia by finding only six cells and that he had been moved to the ICU because in order to start chemotherapy treatment, he would have to be on dialysis for his failing kidneys—but Nic had lived!

Finally, I was able to send Nic's phone charger up to his room, and he was able to call me and tell me all that had transpired that evening. We had gone down to Texas with the understanding that Nic had been diagnosed with lymphoma. However, after running some tests, the doctor discovered that Nic had a very rare lymphatic leukemia that was usually a childhood sickness. Not only that, but it just so happened that the on-call doctor was a world-renowned specialist in that kind of cancer and that they had all the specialized medicine for him on hand. God is big like that! Had we waited until Nic's appointment, we might not have had the correct doctor.

It was a very difficult first week of treatment and dialysis, but Nic continued to be in good spirits. The nursing staff was always so surprised that he was up and talking to them and smiling; most people in the intensive care unit were not so chipper. Seven days after his treatment started, a scan was done to see if the treatment was having any effect on the tumors. To the surprise of everyone, the scan could find no cancer in my husband's body! Again, God is big like that!

The oncologist explained that we would have to continue with some sort of treatment to make sure the cancer stayed gone, but there was an uncommon opportunity for us to consider. He explained that they did not run trials on children and because this was a childhood cancer, there was not much study and trial medication that could be used to see if there was a better treatment plan for treating kids. Nic, however, was an adult, and as an adult, he could choose to do a trial that could possibly help doctors come up with a better and quicker way of treating these kids. The only other man that had been diagnosed with this was a football player in the NFL, and he had done the trial, which was very physically rough, but he was back playing in the league again already. I knew my husband and his heart for kids, and I knew he would say yes to the trial.

"If the devil is going to drag us into hell, we might as well plunder it and take these kids out with us!" became our battle cry.

My husband would have to stay in the hospital for the next thirty days at least, and I could not even go see him at all because of COVID. The thought of leaving him down there was too overwhelming for me, so my spiritual father flew down to Texas to get me. After visiting his son for a few days, who was about an hour outside of Houston, and with Nic moved out of the intensive care unit, I was ready to go home and see my kids. I and my spiritual father flew home together, and I headed home to my kids. They were happy to see me but heartbroken to realize that their dad would not be home for Christmas.

"We will celebrate when Dad comes home," I told them, and they were willing to wait.

Every time I spoke to Nic during this time, he would tell me of something amazing that had happened. With no one there to visit or come pray for people because of COVID, my husband would walk the halls of the hospital, praying over every room, and soon the nurses were saying how strange it was that there were hardly any patients on a usually packed floor. One time Nic was moved to a room next to the helicopter pad. I remembered hearing that helicopter take off about every thirty minutes. However, when Nic was roomed next to it, that helicopter never took off even once. God is big like that!

Our amazing families stepped up for us a lot during this time. My parents and in-laws helped me so much with my kids and animals. Our church family came alongside us with not only prayers and food, but financially, we were also very well taken care of. People from all over the world were giving to us and praying for Nic and watching our story unfold. The kids' school had a fundraiser to help with the financial side of things, and kids from the school would tell my kids they were praying for them and were there for them if they needed them. I am not sure how we would have done it without all of them. Even Nic's job held his position open for him and kept his office just as Nic had left it. It was truly the hands and feet of God helping us through this time. As always, my amazing Kirste and wonderful friend Gina were there to physically hold my hand through it all.

Now, the matter of our adoption needed to be addressed. The final paperwork had been drafted and was ready for signatures, but we knew we could not sign them without disclosing the situation we now found ourselves in. I had the oncologist write a basic overview of Nic's diagnosis and prognosis, and I wrote a letter explaining what had happened and what we were believing God for in this time.

Our agency explained to us that when you had a major diagnosis like this, it was general policy not to be considered for adoption or be able to hold a foster license for at least five years after clinical remission. However, because we had already been chosen and matched with a family, we had about two weeks to communicate with the family and have them decide whether to continue with the adoption or not. We sent the letter, and it was up to the other family now. They wrote back within just a few days with a resounding, "God is going to heal your husband, and these are your babies!" God is big like that!

On my next visit to Texas, Nic and I signed our final adoption papers. The lady who was our notary was shocked that in the middle of all the chemotherapy and tough times, we would continue to trust God and his promises.

"Stowick, Noble Tekoa, Benaiah, Urijah, Mariah, and Mahalia." I would say their names over and over to remind myself of the vision set before us.

Finally, the kids and I were able to fly to Houston to see Nic in January. That's right; I flew with all four kids by myself on a plane to Houston during the COVID season. Luckily, my kids were awesome and helped me the whole way. It was so great to go pick up the man I was not sure would even come out of the hospital. I remember pulling into the covered parking area and them wheeling him out to me with his month's worth of bags and stuff people had sent him for Christmas. The word *joy* would not be enough to explain it. I could have stood there and hugged him forever, but then the voice of the parking attendant interrupted the moment.

"Please move along; this is not a long-term parking area!" she yelled over all the traffic noise.

Generally, that would have ticked me right off, but I was so excited to drive away from that hospital with my husband that I just jumped in the car and left. He was only out for a few days, and then it was time for treatment again. We had an awesome visit for New Year's, and it seemed to go so quickly. Soon we were in the same parking garage, saying our goodbyes once more. This time it would be for a much shorter amount of time, but it was still very hard. Early that next morning, the kids and I headed back to Colorado.

Soon after that, I was called to Texas to pick Nic back up and bring him home with me. It was so nice to have him home, but I quickly realized that I was no longer just a wife now. I was a caregiver. That was a very hard transition for me to make. I already had four kids, and now I had another person to take care of who was so fragile and could take a turn for the worse at any moment.

The chemotherapy schedule was intense. For five days, Nic would have to be hospitalized and under constant supervision while the medicine was administered. Once his numbers were stable enough, it was then my turn to take care of him. I would take his temperature every two hours to make sure he did not spike a fever. On about day three of being home, he spiked a fever, and off to the emergency room we went. Once we got there, he was admitted for blood cultures and all kinds of tests. He would end up staying there for at least five days again.

When that episode was over, I picked him up, and he was home for another three to four days. These were considered his "good days," where he actually had a bit of an immune system and he could just sleep the whole day to rest up for his next treatment. After that three-to-four-day period, it was time to go back to the hospital for the next treatment, and the whole cycle of treatment, fever, and sleeping started again.

There were so many scary things that happened. During this time, Nic went septic four times. He had an eleven-hour nosebleed that needed medical intervention to stop. If his hemoglobin got too low, he would just pass out with no real warning. The fevers were so terrible; one in particular got up to 110 degrees! Luckily, he was in the intensive care unit already, but the nurses were in total shock because even with his temperature so high, Nic was still chatting and talking with them. He should have been having issues with his brain or dead at that temperature, but God is that good.

Finally, it all came to a head during the eighth treatment out of ten projected treatments. Nic had been so beaten down and sick for so long his body was giving out. Even more than the physical fight, emotionally, he had enough. After hearing that he'd gone septic yet again, he looked over at me from his bed and said, "I am not going to make it this time, babe. I want you to keep living life to the fullest and move on, but I am not going to make it this time."

It was a moment of complete despair for me as I felt like we had finally been released from this part of the journey.

I called all the doctors and said, "Enough. He has had enough, and we will not be moving forward with any more of the experimental treatments. It is time to transition his treatment into the maintenance phase."

They pushed back, wanting him to complete the trial to its fullest extent. However, I knew if he was already accepting death, he would not make it much longer, let alone through two more full treatments.

"Write down that a child would not be able to go through your trial and survive, and take the information you have and be done. As thankful as I am that you have saved Nic this far, I will not stand by and let the medicine kill him," I explained.

The cancer was gone and had been since the seven days in Texas, which had been six months ago; the medicine was killing him at this point. Finally, they agreed and allowed Nic to transition to maintenance. What a relief it was. I was finally seeing glimpses of the man I knew. By June 2021, Nic was confirmed to be in clinical remission. God is awesome like that!

It had been a heck of a journey, and we were ready for a break. There were always more appointments and small setbacks here and there, but imminent death had been vanquished. Yet even here, our family had continued to do normal life things. The kids somehow participated in sports, attended school, went to camps, and lived somewhat normal lives. God is good like that! The valley of the shadow of death was where we had been for so long, yet we were sustained and came through as victors.

Chapter Seven

WE HAD COME through the fire, and God had sustained us. Now it was time to pick things back up and begin to live normally again. The children had weathered the storm so well it was miraculous. Although I had not wanted words like *chemotherapy*, *septic*, and *Daddy is sick* in their lives, as they were in my young life, the Lord held their hearts so well it seemed too good to be true. It was such a sweet and wonderful time of healing for our family. In September, some sweet people gave Nic and me a trip to Mexico for just the two of us. Finally, I felt like a wife again, not just a nurse.

Soon after, we attended a worship night at the church. I was just praying and seeking the Lord when I heard him say, "It's time."

"Time for what, Lord?" I asked.

"It's time for redemption; it is time for new life," He said ever so softly.

I knew right away it was time for us to move forward with bringing our adoptive children into the world. I was not so ready to jump right into the next thing, but after talking with Nic and having another family vote, I knew it was right. The kids were so ready to have a new little baby to love. Honestly, we all needed something to celebrate and look forward to.

November 11 was the day Nic and I headed to the clinic for our frozen embryo transfer. I had started the hormone treatment, which included a couple of pills and an intramuscular shot daily a few weeks earlier. I was already feeling the effects from those, but I think it was just a highly emotional day all the way around.

On the way down to the clinic, the phone rang, and it was our doctor.

"Hello, Kaity. I was just calling to see how you want to do with this, but unfortunately, one of the embryos that we thawed has already passed away. That being said, we do have one that's doing great, but if you want to implant two, we will need to thaw another one."

I instantly burst into tears. How could this be happening? When I adopted six, I planned on six, no matter what the statistics said.

"Yeah, go ahead and thaw another, and we will still implant two," I replied.

"Okay, see you soon, and I am so sorry for your loss. These things do happen, unfortunately," the doctor said compassionately.

I turned to Nic, and we cried together and prayed and knew that our little one would do well in heaven until we got there to see it. We arrived at the clinic, and the transfer procedure went well. I watched on a small television screen as my little embryos moved all around on an ultrasound as they were placed in my body.

"Grow, little ones, grow. Mommy loves you," I said.

A few weeks later, we got the results of my pregnancy test, and it was positive! I was pregnant, but with whom? I went in for an ultrasound, and the doctor said, "Well, there is your little baby right there! Congratulations!"

"Oh, awesome!" I said. "And now the other one?" I waited, hoping that maybe the other baby was just hiding somewhere off-screen, but no.

"Looks like there is just the one, honey," the doctor said. "Again, these things happen."

I was again in a mix of complete joy and overwhelming sorrow. I knew this time I was supposed to have twins and one was not there.

I called Nic and said, "There is just one."

He was as shocked as I was; we were both expecting two.

"Well, honey, we have one here, and that's a miracle! And two or three, we will see when we get up with them, so they are not lost. They just decided to stay home."

I found great comfort in that fact and turned my thoughts to the little one growing inside me. "I think it's Urijah," I told Nic. "I think I am pregnant with Urijah."

"Awesome, babe; we will see when we find out the gender and everything, but I bet you're right," Nic said excitedly.

We had hoped this baby would be a son. It's not that we didn't love all our daughters and our goddaughter, but for the sake of our son, we hoped for a brother for him. Kash had prayed for thirteen years for a brother, and even the foster sibling had added another girl to the herd. Soon, at the gender reveal party, he popped a big balloon, and blue confetti went everywhere! Yes indeed, he had a brother on the way! It was Urijah for sure now. Everyone was over-the-moon excited, and I was full of joy even though I had had the worst morning sickness I had ever experienced a few weeks before.

My pregnancy progressed normally, and we were even able to go visit our goddaughter, who now lived in Atlanta, for spring break. It was an awesome trip. Five days of beaches and sun with all my kids and my husband in one place. God is good like that.

While we walked the beaches, Nic struggled with some terrible back pain. He could not walk very far and would have to sit down. I told him it was probably just weakness from all he had been through, but we would have to get it checked out when we got back home. We said our "see ya laters" and, with many tears, returned home to Colorado from our spring break adventure.

That next week, Nic went to the doctor for a check-up and explained to the doctor about all his pain. After some X-rays and tests, it was determined that Nic was not having back pain but actually hip pain because both of his hips were collapsing. The chemotherapy had caused narcosis in the ball of his hip bones, and part of his bones in both legs was dead. Nic needed double hip replacements.

The first hip replacement was done in May, and amazingly, Nic was up and back to work in just three weeks. That left a few weeks for our goddaughter to come stay with us before the next hip needed to be done, and then, of course, the baby would be here. On Father's Day that year, I began having contractions, and I went to the hospital, where they were able to give me some medications to stop my labor. All my ultrasounds thus far had shown that Urijah was growing very well, so well, in fact, that he was a very big baby for his age.

After I went into preterm labor, they wanted to give me a couple of steroid injections to make sure if he came early, his lungs would be ready for the world. The only drawback was, he could grow even bigger than he was. I wanted the best possible chance for his lungs to be ready, so I got the shots and just prayed he would not be twelve pounds when he finally did come. Our goddaughter stayed with us for eighteen days that summer. God is good like that.

Then it was time for Nic's next hip surgery, and it all went smoothly. A couple of weeks with the walker and then a few with a cane, just like the last one, was what we were expecting.

The kids were participating in the annual rodeo Bible camp that we attended. Nic was still on a walker but healing great. I was still pregnant in the mid-July heat. A few days later, at my son's baseball game, I started feeling contractions again.

Surely not, I thought to myself. *All my babies come late.*

However, a few hours later, I knew it was time to head to the hospital because my son was not going to wait for his due date. It was a long labor, but finally, the time came to push. As they set my son on my chest, I knew he was the biggest baby I had ever had, and I was instantly in love with him, just as all my other children.

"She is bleeding!" I heard the doctor yell.

All of a sudden, I felt cold from the top of my head all the way down my body. I was hemorrhaging. They took my son over to be monitored because he was not breathing well, and I began to go in and out of consciousness. When I would come to again, I would look across the room over all the heads of what seemed like twenty nurses working on me and see Nic standing there, holding his cane.

I can't die! Please, Lord, make the blood stop, I prayed.

Nic came up right next to me, and I asked him to tell it to stop as well. As soon as he did, the blood stopped! I was still in and out of consciousness, but I was no longer bleeding, and they were able to save everything I needed to continue having the rest of my babies. Urijah, on the other hand, was struggling to breathe a lot and was taken into the NICU. They wheeled me in to see my baby a few hours later, and he was hooked up to so many tubes and machines it was too much to handle.

They took me to my recovery room, and I had some extra care that was needed, so I was not able to get up and out of bed at all. Nic slept in the NICU next to Urijah that first night, and I cried alone in my room for everything that had transpired in not only the past hours before but for the years of pain, it seemed. I needed him to be okay, and slowly but surely, he improved.

I was totally fine and was discharged as normal from the hospital, but Urijah had to stay in the NICU a bit longer. So I slept in a reclining chair in the NICU even after everything I had physically gone through the days before, because I would not leave my son. Soon the nurses told me I needed to go home and have a shower and a break. As much as I didn't want to, I knew they were right, so I headed to the house with Nic.

During that car ride, I broke down again.

"What the heck is happening? Why does everything have to be so hard?" I cried to Nic. I continued, "How will I ever give birth to the other three babies we have adopted?"

Nic answered, "That is the point. The enemy doesn't want them to even be born. Think of all the things that have happened since we chose to follow the calling in our lives."

I was shocked by his answer. He was absolutely right. Since we had said yes to God, we had had the house-building fiasco, cancer, near death, and so much hardship.

"It's all worth it," I said. "For Urijah and our goddaughter, it is all worth it."

"Yes, it is," Nic said, and in that moment, we knew, no matter what the enemy had tried or done, God's plan would be done in our lives. Nothing could touch us or kill us or anything else without His hand holding us. We were determined that we would continue the calling, and we would have the rest of our babies no matter what!

That next day, Urijah made an amazing turnaround and headed home to be welcomed by his over-the-moon excited siblings.

Soon I sat with Urijah on my lap at the Hope Haven Rwanda luncheon.

* * *

"Now tell me about yourself, Kaity," a sweet lady said with a big smile on her face.

I told her just a little bit of my story that day but figured I should write the rest down because maybe someone out there needs to know that God is good like that! Maybe someone else needs to know that they can do it!

You can have a difficult childhood, be a teen mom, have challenging marriage experiences, be a single mom, follow the call of God, fight for your husband, raise your kids in struggle, and almost die. However, with God on your side, you can still make it. God is good like that!

Printed in the USA
CPSIA information can be obtained
at www.ICGtesting.com
LVHW010916070823
754250LV00018B/1290